The
DIY COLORING BOOK

**An Adult Do It Yourself Coloring Book
For Anyone & Everyone Who Wants To Be A Coloring Book Artist
(or you can just call it a sketchbook)**

by

Terri Dennis

aka Pop Art Diva

You always wanted to draw your own coloring book

and now you can!

Bored with the gazillion coloring books on the market? Tired of just adding color to someone else's art? Have your own artistic vision for mandalas, fairies, dragons, cats, dogs, ocean creatures, flowers, landscapes, secret gardens, patterns, holidays, inky doodles, fantasy drawings and zentangles?

Maybe you just want to doodle without being told where to doodle. You're a creative maverick, you don't want to be confined inside someone else's design. Here is a pre-formatted, pre-bound already set up for you, blank sketchbook / coloring book just waiting for you to fill it with your own hand drawn art.

All you need is some art supplies and imagination.

Then you get to color it!

INSIDE THIS BOOK

What follows are simply blank pages where you can doodle, sketch and draw to your heart's content. There's no restrictions, no pressure, no expectations and best of all – no lines to get in your way!

A Few Tips:

Not every piece will be a masterpiece, don't worry. Most artist's sketchpads are usually a big mess. They're filled with unfinished doodles, drawings with boo-boos, big x's over things the artist didn't like and, often a few comments (some not fit to print) and notes for their final drawings. Take a look at Rembrandt's sketches sometime. Don't let the blank white page intimidate you! Just put your pen to paper and start because as every journey starts with the first step, every drawing begins with the first line.

Check out "Zentangle" on Google. It's the art of creating beautiful images from repetitive pattern.

Start with geometric designs before you try to tackle drawing "things". It will build your confidence and you might love the abstract designs you create.

Nobody, *artists included,* can draw a straight line without a ruler. Straight lines are boring anyway.

Relax and let the drawing take you where it wants to go. Draw a squiggle or a doodle and look at it for a bit, let it talk to you. If it's not speaking, draw another squiggle. If it's still not talking, connect the two squiggles … do this enough and bingo, you have a doodle before you! Check out some of the videos of my zendoodles on my Facebook page: http://facebook.com/ColoringLifeHappy for examples!

Put the coffee cup on another table, trust me.

What are you waiting for? Buy this DIY Coloring Book and start drawing!

DEDICATION

TO ALL THOSE WHO LOVE ART, BUT ESPECIALLY, TO THE ARTISTS

"EVERY ARTIST WAS FIRST AN AMATEUR." - RALPH WALDO EMERSON

To become an artist one must simply begin to create art. That being said, by creating art you are not automatically a *professional* artist. A professional artist is someone who makes part or all of their living creating art of one form or another. Full time professional artists make their *entire* living from their art. Some full time professional artists work for a company, some freelance as self-employed artists who take on projects and commissions from more than one client.

To become a *professional* artist one must have more than talent and a desire to create. Training, education, dedication and discipline are companions to that desire. Without those elements art remains a hobby, not a profession. There is nothing wrong with having art as a hobby, in fact it's a good thing which can give a person many years of satisfaction and joy. And, like the quote above says, every professional was an amateur first. But make no mistake about it, *professional art* is hard work and anyone who says it's not is doing it wrong.

Additionally, and contrary to popular myth, professional artists are not just happy-go-lucky free spirits, unencumbered by life's realities. Professional artists have mortgages, family responsibilities and life problems just like anyone else. People who make their living as *freelance artists* deal with those life requirements and also must deal with clients as well as the responsibilities of any corporation or business enterprise. A successful freelance artist is not only a creative individual following their passion but a multi-level executive with knowledge of all the elements of modern business. Just like any other business, those self-employed in the art field must also deal with government licenses, taxes, bookkeeping, budgets and all the other day to day challenges of a working business concern. For those artists who make use of the internet, theft of their work is another day to day challenge as anyone with an internet connection can download their images with the click of a mouse and attempt to use that pirated art without payment or authorization, even despite copyright notices. Sometimes being a professional artist can take all the fun out of art but we do it because we love it, because we are compelled to create and because we want to share it with the world however we can. It's what artists do – and usually while splattered from head to toe in whatever medium we're working in that day.

This book is dedicated to all the great professional artists – employed and freelance - out there who have spent a lifetime learning and applying their craft. Here's to the years and small fortunes they have spent on art education and supplies, to the thousands upon thousands of hours creating, the midnight oil burned while meeting a deadline, the meals and family activities missed to finish a piece of artwork on time, the sigh of relief when a piece is finished and ready to give to the customer or client .... just before the cat, dog or child runs by and knocks a cup of coffee all over it.

I salute you, my brothers and sisters in the arts, and tip my ink pens, brushes and pencils to you all.

Terri, aka Pop Art Diva

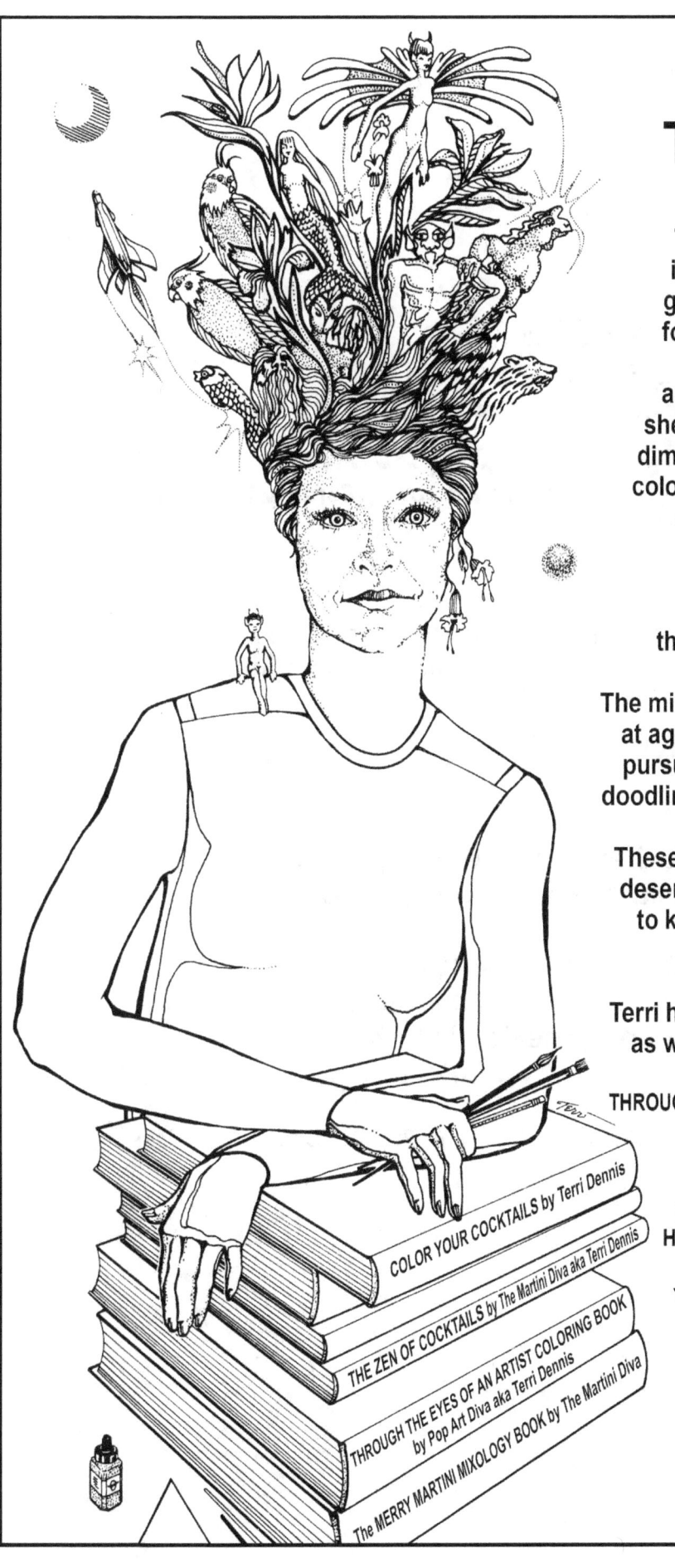

ABOUT
THE AUTHOR

Terri Dennis, aka Pop Art Diva, is a professional illustrator and graphic artist/designer with over four decades of work experience in the publishing, advertising and marketing fields. In that time she has worked in every type of two dimensional media including pastels, colored pencils, markers, pen and ink, oils, acrylics and watercolors. Her favorite art mediums these days are colored pencils and watercolors with the occasional foray into acrylics.

The minute she was handed her first crayon at age five, Terri dedicated her life to the pursuit of creativity, color and the joy of doodling, drawing, illustration and painting.

These days she doodles and draws in the desert town of Tucson, Arizona and tries to keep her cat, Bailey, from eating or spilling stuff on her art.

Terri has published several cocktail books as well as 3 coloring books, including:

THROUGH THE EYES OF AN ARTIST COLORING BOOK
The ZEN of COCKTAILS
COLOR YOUR COCKTAILS
MANDALAS & MOTIVATION
MERRY MARTIN MIXOLOGY BOOK
HALLOWEEN MARTINIS & MUNCHIES

You can find her other creative works at:
PopArtDiva.Com
ShopPopArtDiva.Com
MartiniDivaBoutique.Com
MartiniDiva.Com
TheMartiniDiva.Com

This book is a
COLORING LIFE HAPPY PRODUCTION
produced and published by
ColoringLifeHappy.Com
Coloring Pages, Posters, Cards, Clothing, Decor & More by PopArtDiva

Join Terri on Facebook for Art and Coloring News, Tips, Videos, Free
Coloring Pages and fun art industry tidbits and humor at:

Facebook.com/ColoringLifeHappy

Share your drawings, colorings and
come chat with Terri aka PopArtDiva on Social Media:

Twitter.com/PopArtDiva
Twitter.com/Normlchallenged
Twitter.com/TheMartiniDiva
Instagram.com/themartinidiva